GW00578116

STORRINGTON IN PICTURES
Yesterday & Today

Frontispiece: Street scene in Storrington, 1921

STORRINGTON IN PICTURES

Yesterday & Today

Joan Ham

Phillimore

1979

Published by
PHILLIMORE & CO. LTD.
London and Chichester
Head Office: Shopwyke Hall,
Chichester, Sussex, England

ISBN 0 85033 319 9

Printed in Great Britain by
UNWIN BROTHERS LIMITED
at The Gresham Press, Old Woking, Surrey
and bound by
THE NEWDIGATE PRESS LTD.
at Book House, Dorking, Surrey

DEDICATION

To my dear, patient and encouraging husband, who has watched this project grow and who has helped it by transporting me to the further outposts of the parish—with my love and thanks

Illustrations

Acknowledgments

This book has been made possible by the residents of Storrington, some of whom have spent their whole lives here and knew the village in very different times. Whenever I have asked them to delve into their memories, or their souvenirs and pictures, I have met with unfailing enthusiasm, helpfulness and often suggestions to 'go and speak to so-and-so, who knows all about . . .' whatever I am looking for. So the fascinating trail has led me from one to another of Storrington's 'old inhabitants', and I have learnt a great deal about the vanished village that was here between the wars and much earlier.

It would be most ungrateful of me not to acknowledge such a great debt, and to thank them all for their patience and their help. Indeed, I am most happy to have the opportunity to do so.

Two ladies have been positive mines of information — Miss Florence Greenfield and Mrs. Elizabeth Whitbourne. One of the first questions any researcher in this field is asked, is 'Have you talked to Miss Greenfield?' I have, and I am delighted to be able to thank her for all the help she has given. Mrs. Whitbourne grew up in the old Rectory, later the Council Offices — her father, grandfather and brother have all been 'Rev. Faithfull's — and I had the pleasure (with the kind co-operation of Mr. E. Davis) of exploring the building from attics to cellars with Mrs. Whitbourne, and learning all about it. I have also received much information and many pictures from her which is all much appreciated.

Others who have helped me have been Miss O. Towse (whose family had the butcher's shop in Church Street, later Selden's); Miss Q. Hecks whose family farmed at Sullington and brought the first electricity to the village; Miss E. Moon whose family were millers and bakers at Chantry and Sullington Mills; Miss A. Rapley, Miss Clark-Williams, Miss B. Goldsmith, Mrs. P. Searle, Miss E. Howard, Mrs. Howell, Mrs. Bowles, Mr. and Mrs. Melhuish, Mrs. Attwater, Mrs. Bowley, Miss M. Wright and Mrs. Bickworth, Mrs. E. Barnard, Mr. K. Hills, Mrs. D. Gill, Mrs. D. Line and Miss A. MacDonald.

In addition, thanks are due to Mr. Scotcher for the information provided in the caption to plate 123; to Mrs. P. Fradd and Miss T. Wallis Myers for plate 162; to Beckett Newspapers Ltd., for plates 188-192, 197 and 225. Plate 180 is reproduced by courtesy of J. Armour-Milne.

Lastly, but by no means least, I would like to thank Rev. J. Norman who kindly allowed me to photograph the old paintings in the Rectory and to take photographs inside the Parish Church, and Father Cassidy, C.R.P., and the Prior, Father Joyes, C.R.P., for information and permission to take photographs inside the Catholic Church.

Storrington Parish

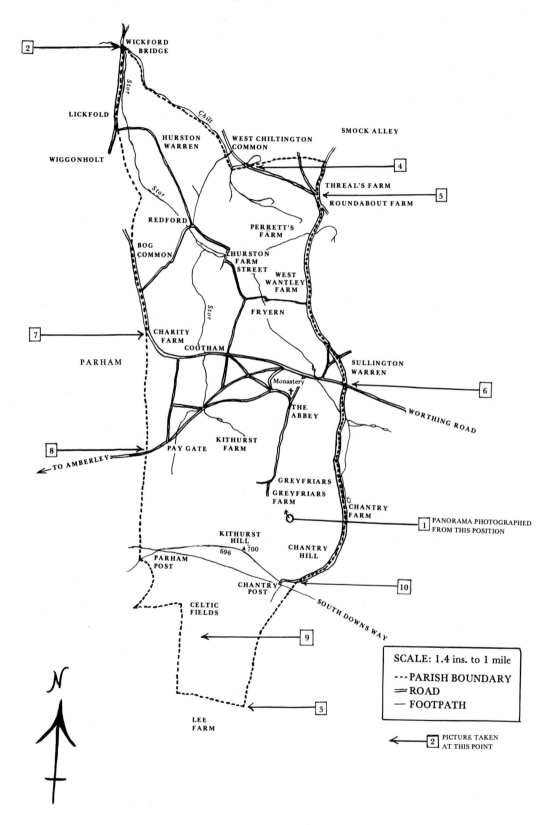

WICKFORD BRIDGE

2

Stor

Chilt

LICKFOLD

HURSTON WARREN

WEST CHILTINGTON COMMON

SMOCK ALLEY

WIGGONHOLT

4

THREAL'S FARM

ROUNDABOUT FARM

5

Stor

REDFORD

PERRETT'S FARM

BOG COMMON

HURSTON FARM STREET

WEST WANTLEY FARM

Stor

FRYERN

CHARITY FARM

7

COOTHAM

PARHAM

Monastery

SULLINGTON WARREN

6

WORTHING ROAD

THE ABBEY

KITHURST FARM

8

PAY GATE

TO AMBERLEY

GREYFRIARS

GREYFRIARS FARM

CHANTRY FARM

1 PANORAMA PHOTOGRAPHED FROM THIS POSITION

KITHURST HILL

696   700

CHANTRY HILL

PARHAM POST

CHANTRY POST

10

CELTIC FIELDS

SOUTH DOWNS WAY

9

3

LEE FARM

SCALE: 1.4 ins. to 1 mile
- - - PARISH BOUNDARY
═══ ROAD
── FOOTPATH

2 PICTURE TAKEN AT THIS POINT

N

The Parish

INTRODUCTION

James Dallaway described Storrington in 1819 as a small market town lying seven and a quarter miles North-east of Arundel:

> 'The parish is irregularly shaped, being of a greater length than width, and contains collectively 2,907 statute acres, thus distributed — arable and pasture 1,738, down 707, common 236 and in Hurston Warren 226 acres.'

We are also told that Storrington:

> '. . . consists of a long street, with another diverging about the centre, at right angles: A turnpike road from Stopham Bridge to join the road from Worthing to Horsham at Washington Common, was made in 1810, and passes through this town. An act for making a turnpike road to join the parish road from Arundel to Chichester, passed in 1812.'

R. L. Hayward, writing his valuable handbook to the village and church, notes that there were 132 houses in Storrington in 1801, and one more was added in the next 10 years. The following decade saw the building of 39 new houses.

We have lived in this parish for a quarter of a century, and the pace of life and growth of the area has escalated like a chain reaction in that time. Many fields and open spaces that we enjoyed when we moved in, are now densely packed estates of council and private houses. Buses that stopped in the Square outside our shop in the early years, first disappeared into a small bus station at the east end of the village, and now circle around a large terminus behind the old shopping centre. The character of the main High Street has changed beyond belief.

It was the gradual disappearance of the village into which we moved, that prompted me to place on record a few of those changes, before they too are lost for all time.

It seemed a good idea to begin as James Dallaway did, by circumscribing the parish of today, but in keeping with this book, to do so in pictures. Here, then, in 1979 is Storrington.

1. This panorama of Storrington was photographed in the Spring of 1977 from the old Roman terraceway that curves around the shoulder of the hill from Chantry Post, and looks north-west.

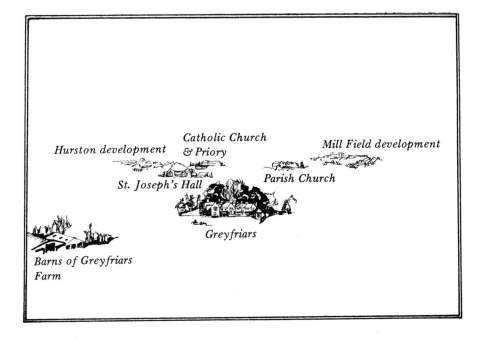

2. **Wickford Bridge.** This is the most northerly part of the parish. The small bridge, built on a sharp bend and crossing the Stor, is a frequent traffic casualty — as can be seen by the temporary rail on the left, where the parapet has been knocked over again. This road connects us with Pulborough. The new link, built to straighten a bend in the road just past the visible road in the picture, revealed the site of a Roman bath house. The eastern edge of the floors had been washed away by the Stor over the years.

3. **Near Lee Farm.** This is the most southerly point, the opposite end to the last picture and possibly the most peaceful. It lies in the Downs, S.W. of Chantry Post. In the middle distance are the only living creatures — our traditional sheep.

4. (*opposite page*) **Munckmead.** This little river is the Chilt and marks, at this point, the East-West boundary of the parish. A little further on, the river is joined by another small tributary and makes a right-angled turn North-West, carrying the parish boundary with it to join the North-South boundary at Wickford Bridge. Near the bridge, the Chilt and the Stor join to flow in a common stream to pour into the Arun at Pulborough. On the opposite side of the road from the place where this picture was taken is Munckmead pond; the river has just flowed underneath the road at this spot. A Roman road which connected with Stane Street also crossed the present main road at this point, travelling South-West.

5. **Peacock Tree.** The junction of four roads between West Chiltington and Storrington is nearly at the N.E. boundary point of the parish.

6. **Worthing Road (Sullington), Three Gates.** Storrington meets its eastern neighbour along one of its long boundaries. At this point, the main road to Washington bisects both parishes.

7. **Charity Farm.** Where the parish boundary, the main road to Pulborough, and the Parham estate wall meet in the west of the parish, is this quaintly-named farm, still known to many older folk as 'Bread Farm'. Charities were founded in 1779 and 1806 to supply bread to the poor not receiving parish relief. It was distributed in church. This land was given to provide the money for the bread.

Amberley Road. At this point the main road to Amberley crosses the parish boundary almost at right-angles. This beautifully straight road began as a turnpike in 1819 (the one mentioned in the Act of 1812 which Dallaway noted). The cottage known as 'Paygate' at the junction of Amberley Road and Clay Lane was the old toll-house.

9. **Celtic Fields.** In the S.W. end of the parish, high up in the downs, the long shadows of lynchets betray the presence of our pre-Roman ancestors. They ploughed and cropped this area of the hills, and after centuries of sheep-rearing, the post-war inhabitants of the area returned to arable farming and cattle-raising.

10. **Chantry Post.** The view taken from this well-known landmark on the South Downs Way shows our S.W. boundary. It coincides very neatly with all of the visible road. Storrington lies to the left and Sullington to the right of this road.

Then and Now

11.   Storrington in the 1880s

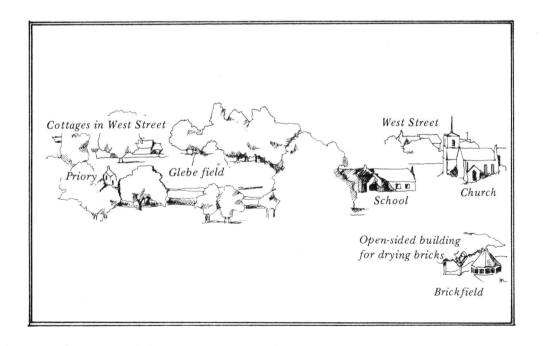

Cottages in West Street

West Street

Priory

Glebe field

School

Church

Open-sided building
for drying bricks

Brickfield

12. Storrington after 1934

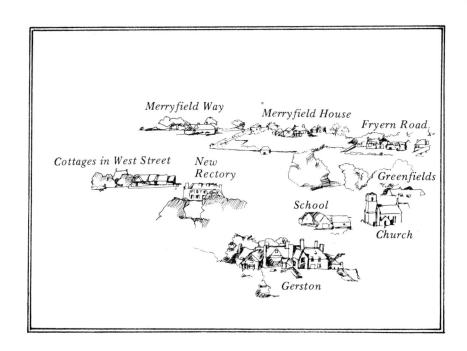

Merryfield Way   Merryfield House   Fryern Road

Cottages in West Street   New Rectory   Greenfields

School   Church

Gerston

13. **Storrington 1977**

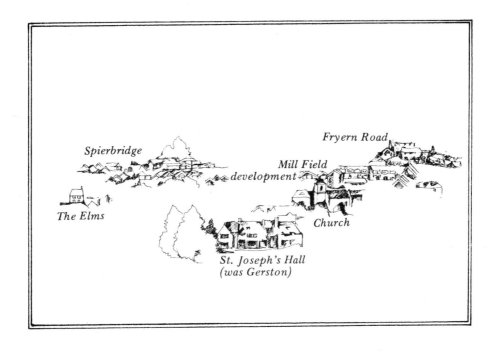

The Parish Church

14. **Eastern Aspect of Storrington Church, 1841.** This painting by Sco hangs in the Rectory, and there is a copy in the church. It shows the profile of the church before the S. aisle was built. Storrington had a church in 1068 which was mention in Domesday Book and walls of thi original church are on the N.E.

15. **Eastern Aspect of Storrington Church, 1977.** This view is taken from the same point (now the Abbey garden). The screen of trees has gone, to reveal the north aisle on the right. The chancel has been lengthened and its roof raised — this was part of the alterations of 1873, which later included the new south aisle (left) and the vestry.

16.   **Storrington Church before 1876.** A much simpler church with just the central nave, tower and north aisle (unseen here). The door in the tower is the main entrance to the church, and there was a floor above for the bell-ringers. The south side of the churchyard was used for burials — tombstones can be seen all around.

17.   **Storrington Church, 1879.** After re-opening in 1876, following the addition of the south aisle, which meant that some tombstones had to be moved. These can be seen leaning against the wall.

18. **Storrington Church before 1921.** View taken from land opposite the south side of the church called the Bell Acre The new south aisle is clothed with creeper.

19. **Storrington Church, 1977.** This was taken from the garden of The Horsecroft.

20. Storrington Church. This is the aspect from further south on the Bell Acre. To the right can be seen the roof and chimney of The Horsecroft, and to the left, a cottage and the school.

21. Storrington Church, 1977. The same viewpoint as the roof of The Horsecroft, and the school roof (now a Youth Club) shows. Now, the yew trees in the churchyard are mature, and the foreground is the car parking area for the tennis courts.

22. Storrington Church and Meadow, 1927. This view from the north-east shows part of the churchyard and the church meadow. This meadow was consecrated in 1927.

23. Storrington Church, 1977. The consecrated meadow now has graves in it. The young trees of the previous picture screen much of the church.

24.   **Chancel Arch of the Parish Church.** This was built in 1873 when the chancel was extended by about nine feet. The two texts painted around the outside read: 'The word was made flesh and dwelt among us. Alleluia' and 'The palace is not for man but for the Lord God.' The pulpit is of Caen Stone and carved with the figures of the apostles.

25.   **Chancel Arch, 1977.** The texts have now been painted out, the outer one first and the inner one in 1928. The ornate altar of the earlier picture has gone — it was installed in the Lady Chapel in 1928 during alterations. The pulpit has also been replaced in 1938 by a new one in memory of Mrs. Ravenscroft's parents. Figures from the old stone pulpit are preserved elsewhere in the church.

The Roman Catholic Church

. Old House and Priory, about 1900. his house stood on the site of the oman Catholic Church. To the east is e chapel which was used for worship fore the church was built, and behind the Priory. Before these were built, rishioners attended Mass in the 'Old ouse'. The first six Roman Catholic iests and brothers came to Sand Lodge School Hill and a downstairs room in e house was used as a chapel.

. Priory Church of our Lady of England, 1977. The foundation stone of this Roman Catholic Church was laid by e Bishop of Southwark, Cardinal Bourne, in 1902 on the site of the Old House. This picture was taken from above e shrine in more or less the same position.

28. Roman Catholic Church and Priory, 1907. The church is a mere five years old in this picture, having been added to the priory.

29. Roman Catholic Church and Priory, 1977. The small buildings between the church and priory have given way to the cloisters. At the north-eastern end of the monastery a new hall has been built for public events. It was completed in 1976.

Church of Our Lady of England, Storrington

30. **Sanctuary of the Priory Church before 1955.** The altar is at the far end of the sanctuary against the reredos, and the chair stands to the right. Two angels on plinths frame the arch.

31. **The Sanctuary, 1977.** In common with Catholic churches throughout the country, the altar was moved away from the reredos to a position where the Mass can be celebrated facing the congregation in 1972. The angels have given place to two lecterns, and the chair and servers' stools now occupy a central position below the altar, so that the priest can face the people during the first half of the Mass. New concealed lighting illuminates the sanctuary and the statue above the reredos.

The Rectory

32. **Front Entrance of the Rectory from S.E.** The entrance is through the door in the tower, which leads up a flight of stairs to the front hall. Shrubbery and flower beds edge the wide drive. The turn of the path to the lower left-hand corner leads to the stables, and behind the tower, the path leads to the garden in the next pictures.

33. **Offices of Chanctonbury Rural District Council, 1977.** Where the tower stood, a flight of outside steps leads to the large, imposing front door. To the left can be seen the new south wing, with offices below and council chamber above. The front garden has given way to a hard car park, although formal flower beds are still maintained close to the building. Now there is another change in the wind, as the Chanctonbury R.D.C. is no more, and the future of the building is under debate.

34. The Rectory from the Garden, before 1933. View from the N.W. corner. The lower bay window is the rector's drawing room.

35. Back of the Council Offices, 1977. From the same aspect. The old drawing room now houses the computers which are needed to conduct council business in the 1970s.

36. Rectory from the Garden, before 1933. View from the S.W. corner. This shows a rustic porch and arched doorway leading on to the wide lawns. The tower (*right*) contains the entrance hall.

37. S.W. view of Council Offices, 1977. The rustic porch has been removed, the tower demolished and a new south wing added. A prefabricated hut stands on the old lawns.

Church Street

38. A Pretty Corner of Storrington. The cottage at the right is covered with creeper, and in its old stone walls are three gates. The church can be seen high up on the left, and three fine chestnut trees provide shade in the middle of the road junction.

39. The Church Corner, 1977. The cottage has been enlarged and stripped of creeper. The roofed gate has gone. A traffic island stands in the centre of the road with two saplings — the third died — which replaced the trees. The church is obscured by a mature yew. The new lamp standards have marched up to this part of the village, and there are fewer trees.

40.   Church Street, 1916. Looking towards the south. The rectory wall can be seen, narrowing the road, and some fine chestnut trees in the garden, on the right.

41.   Church Street, 1977. The rectory wall has been set back to contain the car park for the Council Offices. The chestnut trees behind the wall have gone, revealing the Parish Church. The Horsecroft is visible at the junction of Church Street and Greyfriars Lane, beyond the parked cars.

42. **Old Cottages and the Manor House Hotel.** This shows an attractive village street of old cottages and an old country hotel built in 1870 on the site of an older house. It was previously called 'Mount Lodge'. The old cottage beyond the Manor House is 'Stockbury' and was occupied by Mr. Stocker the plumber.

43. **Old Cottages and Stockbury House, 1977.** The old cottages remain, although the end door is now blocked up and out of use. A new lamp-standard rises above the old roof. The Manor House and old Stockbury have gone, and in their place is a development of private flats called 'Manor Court', and further down, Stockbury House — offices and flats. The street is framed by yellow lines, and it is not unusual to find cars parked on the narrow pavement inside them.

44. **Church Street, 1900-1910.** View from slightly further south, showing Orchard Dale next to Georgian House (the Post Office).

45. **Church Street, 1977.** The houses at the end of Church Street on the right are now shops with flats over the top. The horse-and-cart has given way to the motor car.

5. **Church Street, before 1929.** On the left is Georgian House, the Post Office at this time, with telegraph boys standing outside. The Manor House can be seen opposite, and facing into Church Street is The Dawes, later to become the Post Office.

47. **Church Street, 1977.** Georgian House is now screened by a large tree from this viewpoint. On the right the last remaining part of the Manor House garden wall can be seen outside the new flats. An empty space is where The Dawes stood.

48.   **Church Street looking South, 1913.** On the left are some cottages and above them can be seen the upper storeys of the Manor House behind its wall and hedge. Note the shops on the right.

49.   **Church Street, 1977.** The shops on both sides have changed their character and the traffic and yellow lines tell their own story. This is no longer the quiet side-street that led only to the church and the downs.

The Post Office

50. **The Dawes, 1953.** This house in West Street facing south became the Post Office in 1952. It continued in this capacity until demolished in 1958 after the ceiling collapsed. The site was derelict for the next four years, during which time the business of the Post Office was transacted in a building on the site of the garden. The house was originally an inn called *The Swan and Daws*, later *The King's Head*.

51. **The Post Office, 1977.** This was built on the site of The Dawes' garden, the old house having occupied the open site behind the fence in this picture. It opened for business in March 1964. The original entrance was next to the posting box under the sign, but a glass porch and entrance vestibule were later added to the right-hand side.

52. **Junction of West Street, Church Street and the Square, about 1904.** On the left is a garden wall going round the corner to meet Greenfield's shop. In the Square is a small shop, then a three-storeyed house with a tall fascia and a small cottage (a bank) next door. The right-hand corner is lined with houses and small-windowed shops. Between the small bank on the left and the end wall of The Elders is a space, and ponies graze in the meadow behind it.

53. **The Same Junction, 1977.** The boy walking in the road would not survive long in the late 1970s! The corner has a steel barrier to make pedestrians use the crossing, and the traffic shows why. The second building on the right has three shops on the ground floor. The three-storeyed house in the Square has lost its squared fascia and chimney, and acquired two large plate-glass windows for the shop. The church-like cottage next door has become a modern flat-roofed Lloyds Bank, and next to it is The Homestead, built about 1910.

The Square

The Square, 1920s. The three-storeyed house next to F. Stubbs shows signs of the recent alteration to its fascia. small shop window has appeared on the right and a second door on the left. Lloyds Bank has replaced the cottage on right and the *White Horse* sports an A.A. badge.

55. **The Square, 1977.** F. Stubbs has become a Travel Agency — a real sign of the times. The next shop is double-fronted and has lost its second door. *The White Horse Hotel* no longer has its A.A. badge and the horse on its sign-board has turned round! The village Roll of Honour boards of the 1914-18 war, visible on the wall in the last picture, have now gone.

56. **The Square, 1910.** Greenfield's grocery and drapery shop open onto Church Street in this picture, with Mr. Greenfield's house next to it in West Street. The tall white house next to Greenfield's Furnishing Stores is the home of Mr. E. J. Greenfield.

57. **The Square, 1977.** The entire far corner is now one large self-service grocer, Storrington Stores, and has passed out of the Greenfield family. The block facing the Square is also one — Greenfield's ironmongery and wine store. A huge lamp standard soars out of the picture.

58. **The Square before 1900.** On the near-side of *The White Horse Hotel* is the old Market Room with its external stairway. The cornmarket was held here every Tuesday fortnight, and after this ceased, it was let for private functions.

59. **The Square, 1977.** The wall of the Market Room collapsed in Victorian times, and this new frontage was built with an internal staircase before 1900. The door can be seen beside the pedestrian. After World War II it became the headquarters of the W.V.S. and is now a betting shop. Greenfield's extended their grocery shops across the entire lower stories of the houses, and this business is now Storrington Stores.

0. **The Square, 1903.** This west-facing view shows Commercial House, now the large drapery and grocery business of he Flatt brothers. Ten years previously, this building had suffered a disastrous fire. It was extensively rebuilt before the latts took it over, and new shop windows and frontages were put in.

61. **The Square, 1977.** Commercial House now has several shops, beginning with Rosemarie, a dress shop; G. P. O'Connor; Bollom, the dry-cleaners; Graham and Cadell, jewellers and Wilkins the estate agent. Greenfield's ironmongery and wine shop has also spread right across the ground floor of the three buildings at the west end of the Square.

62. **The North Side of the Square, before 1900.** Mulberry House was the home of Charles Botting. In the 1890s his uncle William Bird, who owned the house, left it to Mr. Botting's daughter Ada, who was married to Mr. Tickner, Stationmaster at Pulborough (later at Victoria Station). In 1904, Mrs. Tickner let the house to Capt. Stocker. The road is unmade and looks very muddy in this winter picture.

63. **The North Side of the Square, 1977.** Mulberry House contains offices and the Square itself is a parking zone.

Mulberry House, before 1914. This imposing house in its walled garden faces the Square. It is now the home of Miss [...]tre, and named for the shady mulberry trees in the back garden. The attractive gas lamp standard in the middle of the [...]uare was installed in commemoration of the Jubilee of 1897.

65. **Mulberry House, 1977.** The house, still retaining the old name, is now the offices of Whiteheads, Stuckey Carr & Co., Stubbs & Spofforth. The garden has most of its stone wall, the entrance having been enlarged to give access to the private car park used by the firms in the house. The use of Mulberry House for offices was the work of Mr. Harkiss, an architect, after Miss Petre ceased to live there in 1932.

66. (*above*) **Storrington in the 1920s.** On the left, the tall
creeper-covered shop sells bicycles, and The Homestead
built by Abner Soffe now has a tea garden. At the bottom
of the village is the half-timbered house which he built also
about 1910, and beyond that can be seen Meadowside.
Coming up the street, one passes the cartshed, just beyond
the motor car and the bakery, now run by A. Stillwell,
for the Moons have passed it over to another member of
the family. Commercial House is now Ivens, Kelletts and
Childs, and between the windows are painted signs, 'Boots
and shoes'.

67. **Storrington in the 1950s.** On the left is the High
Street Dairies, the radio and electrical shop of R. Vine
which has lost its creeper-covered fascia and gained a new
shop window. It is interesting to see among the municipal
entertainment adverts on the side wall that the late
Kathleen Ferrier was appearing at the Assembly Hall,
Worthing. The bakery is now run by Hyams, and Commercial House is the showroom for Stocker's Garage. Mr.
Stocker lived in the flat above, and the workshops were
in the yard beside the building.

High Street

8. **High Street, 1910.** The tall shop nearest on the left is E. Coxe the butcher, with separate departments for pork and provisions, and 'meat'. Then comes the little Capital and Counties Bank, followed by The Homestead, which Abner Soffe built between 1907-8, The Elders and the *Half Moon*. On the other side of the yard are the stables. Returning on the other side of the street, we see Eastbrook, built about four years earlier, *The Anchor* and a derelict cottage, and then the blacksmith's just behind the horse and cart.

69. **High Street, 1977.** The passage of time has left many traces. The butcher's shop, after several changes of ownership and frontage is Ham & Knight — radio and electrical shop. The Capital and Counties Bank is a new Lloyds Bank, The Homestead is a sweet and paper shop and The Elders is the Leatherware gift shop. The old stables have become a wine store. The derelict cottage has been demolished and rebuilt as part of *The Anchor*, and the blacksmith's shop has gone.

70. **High Street, 1900.** This pictu[re] taken from further down the stree[t] shows The Elders, with the old lad[y] who lived there. The stables next [to] the *Half Moon* are also easier to s[ee]. The waggons with white hoods are delivering to *The Anchor* from Steyning Brewery, and the neares[t] building on the unpaved side of th[e] road is Moon's bakery and shop, w[ith] their cart shed where the man is standing. Just beyond him is a gentleman's outfitter's. This was before Abner Soffe built his hous[e] beside it.

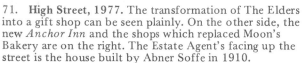

71. **High Street, 1977.** The transformation of The Elders into a gift shop can be seen plainly. On the other side, the new *Anchor Inn* and the shops which replaced Moon's Bakery are on the right. The Estate Agent's facing up the street is the house built by Abner Soffe in 1910.

72. **High Street, before 1906.** Th[e] left side of this west-facing view is unpaved outside the bakery and sh[op]. Next to the *Half Moon* is a pebble cottage with matching wall. The pa[ve]ment is cobbled and the shop on t[he] right in the Square advertises 'Cyc[les] for Hire'. The bus is a Milnes Daim[ler] of *Worthing Motor Services*, and became SD83 for the *Southdown* [in] 1915. Although the postmark on t[he] back of this card was 1914, the sig[n] outside the *Half Moon* says 'J. Bar[nes]'. The amalgamation to King and Barnes did not take place until 19[06].

73. **High Street, 1977.** The bakehouse has been demolished and the pavement set well back. The pebble cottage has become a double-fronted bow-windowed shop selling fancy goods. Its garden wall has gone. The cycle hire shop is now Greenfield's wine store.

4. **Moon's Bakery and Shop, High Street, 1905.** All the people except the driver of the cart are members of the Moon
[fa]mily. The boy with the bicycle has celebrated (1977) his 81st birthday. The little white horse is Joey — he had a long
[lif]e, living in stables behind the bakehouse when not working. His access was through the double doors beside him, and
[hi]s cart was kept in a shed to the left of the bakehouse (not in this picture).

75. **National Westminster Bank, High Street, 1977.** This building was erected on
the site of the demolished bakery in 1958 and the road was set back. The flower
shop and greengrocery reveals the old end wall, where the bakehouse joined it. The
bow windows and shopfronts are new.

Anchor Corner

76. **Worthing Road — School Hill Corner, 1906-7.** Eastbrook on the right is now completed, but the cottage next door is derelict and rat-infested. These rats come from the stream behind the cottage, which also gives its name to Eastbrook. The opposite corner, Star Cottage, has a board in the garden advertising the *Railway Inn*, further up School Hill.

77. **Manley's Hill — School Hill Junction, 1976.** Eastbrook Stores has changed little in appearance, but is now a sports shop. The derelict cottage has gone, and *The Anchor Inn* has taken its place. There is a high sodium street light outside Virginia Cottage.

8. **The Anchor Corner, about 1919.** This view faces west. Outside *The Anchor*, the pavement is cobbled. Beyond the horse and cart is the cartshed, bakehouse and shop. On the other side is the chapel of rest. The stream flows under the road where the brick parapet joins the wall on the right. The horse is pulling a water cart for laying the dust on the roads, and is standing at the stream where the carts were replenished.

79. **Anchor Corner, 1977.** The cobbled pavement has been replaced and edged with double yellow lines. The bakehouse was demolished to make way for new shops and the bank. The old chapel of rest and workshop have gone. The stream now flows under the road in a pipe.

School Hill

80. **School Hill, 1900-1905.** The corner shop on School Hill is a harness-maker. Apart from this corner, the road is unpaved. This view looks up the hill to the north.

81. **School Hill, 1977.** The harness-maker's is now a gentleman's outfitters. A Radio and T.V. shop occupies the site of the garden on the right, and pavement and yellow lines edge both sides of the road.

82. School Hill, 1907. A look at the other side of the road. Mr. Terry's cottage stands by the turning into the yard and Manor Cottage is just visible beyond it.

83. School Hill, 1977. Seventy years on this road is very busy and makes a dangerous corner with the Worthing Road and High Street. Mr. Terry's house and Manor Cottage were demolished and the site is now occupied by the flower beds of the new car park and shopping precinct.

84. School Hill — Mill Lane Junction, 1907. The house on the right is Sand Lodge, which housed the early Catholic fathers before the Priory was built. The protruding sign further up the hill belongs to the *Railway Inn*.

85. School Hill — Mill Lane Junction, 1977. The house on the left has been demolished to make way for a car park, and the tall street-lamps and yellow lines march relentlessly up the hill.

86. Lower End of School Hill, late 1960s. This picture is taken just above Sand Lodge. At the end of the road is Lucking's Gentleman's Outfitters and an old cottage. Then there is an opening leading into School Hill Garage and Mason's cycle shop. Then comes the Dairy and their stores and flat above. Almost out of the picture on the right is Manor Cottage.

87. Lower End of School Hill, 1977. Taken from the same spot, this picture reveals the developers' ruthless hand. Only Lucking's and the attached cottage remain. The garage and cycle shop, the cottages including Manor Cottage have been swept away to make a parking lot for the new shopping precinct. Mill Lane, where the car is coming from, is now blocked off to traffic from this end — the car is coming from the car park. Double yellow lines edge the pavements.

88. School Hill, between 1880-1910. This view is just above the junction with Mill Lane. The interesting thing is the signboard on the right proclaiming *The Railway Inn*. It is a beer-house opened after 1880 and existing as such until after the turn of the century. Plans had been submitted for a railway from Pulborough to Steyning, and it was to run through Storrington with a station near the top of this hill, but cost and opposition defeated the scheme

89. School Hill, 1977. The old *Railway Inn*, now a veterinary practice, has acquired a bow window. A new house can be seen at the top of the hill on the left, on a piece of land where Wickers used to store building materials.

0. **School Hill, 1904.** This view looking south reveals a fine prospect of the downs. The nearest house with the bay windows was Bine Villa, where there was a school for young ladies. The other house with bay windows by the horse and cart (Chilmark) was the home of an Oxford tutor who had several boys there for private tutoring. One of his pupils was the late Duke of Norfolk.

91. **School Hill, 1977.** The road is paved on both sides and the downs are partially obscured by trees and development up the hill on the left. In the field on the left the new fire-station has been built.

Worthing Road

92. **Worthing Road, 1912.** The little shop 'N. Mitchell' is a dressmaker's shop run by the lady standing outside (Mrs. Boorer). In the garden of the cottage opposite is a fine monkey-puzzle tree, which later vanished; the attractive gas-lamp also disappeared, as did the tree at the entrance drive to Brook House.

93. **Manley's Hill, 1976.** The dressmaker's shop is now Eastbrook Stores. The hill is framed by double yellow lines and sodium lamps. The busy traffic tells its own story of change.

94. **Chantry Cross-Roads, 1930s.** This quiet spot on the main road to Worthing is lined with tall pine trees. One of the village wheelwrights has his forge where the cart is parked.

95. **Chantry Cross-Roads, 1977.** The road is now paved and the trees on the right are fewer. On the left the whole corner of Chantry Lane has been cleared, revealing the houses at the lower end of the hill. The quiet Chantry Lane leading to the downs now needs a 'Stop' sign coming into the main road from the hill, and at the entrance to Nightingale Lane opposite is a 'No Entry' sign. This was made necessary by the School Hill crossroads at the other end — an accident black spot.

96. View from the Worthing Road, In the 1920s. This lovely view to the downs, spanning Sullington Hill to Chantry Po
is preserved across an unfenced field bordering the main Worthing Road. There has been a change from sheep-farming to
arable, and the scrub has invaded the smooth slopes of the hills in the later picture. To the extreme left of the 1977 pict
(*below*) is a new building. Behind the lambing pen (*above*) is one of Mr. Bernard Heck's electricity poles — the national
press reported that he was one of the first farmers to use electricity for lighting lambing pens. He generated it from a
turbine installed in Chantry Mill, using water power.

97. View from the Worthing Road, 1977.

Chantry Lane

HANTRY WATERFALL

The Waterfall, in the 1900s. Some things change very little. This lovely waterfall which helps our little river Stor on way from the spring-fed ponds just beyond the brow of the hill is one of them. Sheena Buss and Pippy in the lower ture, however, are very much 1977, whilst the elegant onlooker in the older picture lived in a more leisured time, and uld not have had to take refuge in the side of the road for frequent traffic. Pippy, much to her disgust, must stay on lead until she reaches a field or the top of Chantry Hill.

99. The Waterfall, 1977.

Chantry Mill

VIEW AT CHANTRY MILL, STORRINGTON.

100. **Entrance to Chantry Mill.** After joining the millpond behind Chantry Mill the water pours over some steps at the side into a pool, then flows under this brick arch to run beside the road as the Stor again. There were two manors mentioned in Domesday Book, one having two mills and the other, one. These would have been water-mills, and situated somewhere along the course of the Stor, but their exact position is not known. They would have been very much simpler, possibly little more than a wheel and its associated mechanism in some kind of simple shelter.

101. **Entrance to Chantry Mill, 1977.** The wildness has been tamed and the entrance fenced along the roadside. Now, this area round the pool and stream is a lovely marsh garden which is a delightful sight in the Spring.

02.   **Chantry Mill, 1880s.** In the loading doorway half way up the wall on the right, two of the millers can be seen.

103.   **Chantry Mill, 1977.** The small building in the middle has been raised to the roof level of its neighbour by the addition of a second storey. Its barn door is now a window, as is the loading door of the next building.

104. This is what it would have looked like to have driven into the mill entrance in the 1890s, through the hens wandering about, and past the dog kennel and occupant.

105. The small building has been raised by the 1890s, but is still a windowless barn.

106. Now in 1977, the barn has been converted into living accomodation and has handsome windows. The 'horsepower' is mechanised.

CHANTRY MILL POND #7

107.   **A Walk Round the Millpond.** This was probably taken before the 1920s. The main building on the right is the one that had the roof of the adjoining barn raised. The line of vertical brickwork shows the alteration, and the windows have not yet been added. The structure in the retaining wall of the pond is the top of the steps where water overflows down to the pond, seen earlier at the entrance. The view is to the N.E.

108.   1977. Many more trees hide the hills behind the mill. The new windows in the barn extension can be seen in the end of the left-hand building. The tall door has also been made into a window.

ANTRY MILL STORRINGTON

109.   From the Opposite Side of the Pond, 1909.

110.   1977. The new windows look across the pond, but on the far side (behind the photographer) they now see the back of the Marley Tile Works which adjoin. The small right-hand building almost hidden by a tree in the earlier picture was demolished after the tree crashed through its roof.

.   **Chantry Mill and Pond after 1921.** The pole is a support for electricity wires. Mr. B. Hecks took out the mill-wheel
921 and used the mill to generate electricity from a turbine. This supplied his farmyard and lambing pens and milking
ls at first, and was gradually carried to customers in the village. He was one of the first farmers to use electricity for
king, and the story was interesting enough to appear in national newspapers of the day. The shed mentioned in the
ious picture is seen here more clearly.

.   **1977.** The electricity installation has gone, together with the tall door and the shed.

113. **The Black Mill, before 1923.** This stood in Kithurst Lane, and the view is towards the east. To the right is the Roman Catholic Church. This was the last working windmill in Storrington, and was demolished in 1923.

114. (*below*) **The same site, 1977.** After the demolition of the mill, a house was built on the site. This is Cherry House and its front step is one of the old millstones. There are others serving similar purposes around the house. The Catholic Church is nearly hidden by the tree on the right, but it is clear that we are looking at the same viewpoint.

Greyfriars Lane

15. **The Gate of the Abbey, before 1970.** The beautiful arched gateway of the Abbey, and its pillared stone wall along Greyfriars Lane. The wall, as can be seen, has a pronounced lean outwards, possibly aggravated by the fact that the garden on the inside is level with the top of the wall.

116. **The Abbey Gate, 1977.** This is the rebuilt gate after a lorry stuck in the old one and caused the arch to collapse about 1969-70. Later, the garden wall fell into the lane and was rebuilt without its pillars. A 'No Through Road' sign has been erected at this point, but car drivers still mistake the lane to the Downs for the Amberley Road junction on their maps.

117. **The Abbey, about 1915.** This lovely house was never an Abbey. In 1621, the Rev. Walter Mattock built a rectory which is thought to have been south of this house (*right*) and reached through the existing farm gate opposite Deyneco. In 1871-2, the Rev. George Faithfull pulled down the remains of the old rectory and used the stones to build this house. It became a private house in 1880, and the pupils of the rector nicknamed it 'The Abbey'. The Rev. G. Faithfull moved to the rectory in Church Street (later the Council Offices) from 1880-1934, and The Abbey was let. The tenant in 1900 was Mr. Trotter. He built Gerston and moved there, and The Abbey was then sold to Mr. Bethell in 1911, who made some additions. In the early 1920s he sold it to Col. Ravenscroft, who added the ballroom and music room on the right in 19. In the 1950s, after Col. Ravenscroft's death, the building was sold again and became a Dominican Convent and boarding school. Since this time, as this 1977 picture shows (*below*), there have been many more additions.

118. **The Abbey, 1977.**

119. (*left*) **Smugglers Hut, 1904.** This old cottage in Greyfriars Lane has much curious architecture. It is thought to have an underground tunnel at the back travelling in a westerly direction.

120. (*below*) **Smugglers Hut, 1977.** The ricketty porch has been built in solidly with the house and an upper dormer added beside the chimney. The northern end of the cottage has been considerably rebuilt and new windows look out onto a fine garden. Fresh paint and a tiled roof complete the job of reconstruction, and the cottage is now the home of Mr. and Mrs. Melhuish.

121. (*left*) **Greyfriars Lane.** This picture was taken in the second decade of this century. It shows the southern end, where the lane leads up to footpaths and the downs. The pumping station can be seen below the chalk pit. Drilling for water began here in 1911, and Storrington got its first mains water in 1914. A fine footpath can be seen climbing the downs on the right.

122. (*right*) **Greyfriars Lane, 1977.** The sunlit patch of grass below and to the left of the chalk-pit marks the levelled site of the old pumping station, demolished in 1958. Only an underground reservoir remains, after the new pumping station was built at Smock Alley. The downs cannot be seen here for woods, and even the chalkpit is almost hidden.

123.   **Coldharbour Cottage.** This old cottage is typical of 16th-century building, and the steep pitch of the roof suggests that it was originally thatched. The two outhouses built on the ends were added when the cottage was converted into two. A farm track, visible on the near side of the gate, connected it with Kithurst. The belt of trees on the hillside marks the springline, where the lower chalk meets the upper greensand and the springs and rivers emerge. This is also the level (further to the left of this picture) where the old pumping station was built.

124.   **Coldharbour Cottage, 1977.** Once again the building is one cottage. It stands at the end of a grassy footpath, a popular walk to the downs or back to Kithurst. The downs are covered with many more trees and bushes.

Brown's Lane

125. (*above*) **In the 1900s.** This peaceful rural scene is difficult to relate to the next pictures, but is taken from practically the same spot. It used to be called East Town Lane, and separated farmland on the left from allotments on the right. One of the trees on the right, an oak-tree, survived the development of the area.

126. (*right*) **Winter of 1963.** During this very severe winter when snow lay on the ground for eight weeks, the oak-tree stands out well.

127. **1967.** The only remaining thing from the 1900s is the oak tree. The council houses were built in 1958 and the bungalows behind the fences on the left were built in 1960. The farmland to the left, beyond the pedestrians, was developed in the mid-60s.

West Street

128. West Street, 1930s. Next to the little shop on the right is 'Banksia', once 'Bank House'. The tax supervisor used to live there. Next comes a row of cottages where Mr. Dibble the baker and his daughter, Mrs. Simpson, lived and before them, the baker's shop at the end was run by Mr. Joyes. The large barn was where sacks of flour were kept, having been delivered from the mill behind the village (the Bine-Mill).

129. 'Snobby' Stringer. This little shop was one of four cottages in West Street next to the *Cricketers*, going westwards. Between this and the *Cricketers* was a narrow twitten leading to Twitten Cottage. The older picture of West Street (*above*) shows the top windows of this cottage standing open (next to the *Cricketers*) and also the doorstep. In the 1977 picture, the light on the pavement at this point shows that it is no longer standing. Mr. Stringe is very recognisable later on, (see plate 176) in the picture of servicemen of the First World War posed with the Roll of Honour.

130. (*below*) **West Street, 1977.** The garden fences and creepers on the house-fronts have disappeared. Enormous sodium street lamps march down the road and the ubiquitous yellow lines.

131. West Street, 1841. Photograph of a watercolour by Scott. The cottages in the lower right-hand corner of the picture are opposite to Rose Cottage (first on the left) which was re-named Stone House in the 1960s.

132. **West Street.** The old cottages in the corner of the previous picture are in the middle, with the Village Hall next to them, built in 1894 on land given by the Rector. The Elms, just visible behind the tree on the left, is a laundry in 191

133. **West Street, 1977.** All the old cottages beyond the Village Hall have now been demolished. On the left, the first building past the tree is Colwell's second-hand shop, which has been joined onto Stone House. Next to that is The Elms, also seen in the oldest picture.

The Village Pond

134. **Village Pond and Part of Storrington Common, 1841.** Photograph of a watercolour by Scott. The land on the right is called 'Allotment for recreation' on an inclosure map of 1851. This painting, together with the painting of West Street and the Parish Church, now hangs in the Rectory.

135. **The Village Pond.** The Pulborough Road can be seen at the top right; the pond lies beside it. The picture was taken sometime between 1920 and 1930.

136. The Village Pond, 1977. The pond has been cleaned and kerbed, and trees now screen the house at the end. The recreation ground, beyond the cars on the right occupies the 'Allotment for recreation' of the old map.

137. Storrington Pond, 1909. During the hard winter of this year, the pond froze over so hard that skating was possible. The houses at the other side of the pond are on the Amberley Road. The downs should be visible from this viewpoint, but are blotted out by the weather conditions.

138. Storrington Pond, 1977. This view also looks across the pond towards the Amberley Road. The pond is screened from the houses on the road by tall trees and it can be seen that there are many more houses.

Cootham

9. **The Long Row in the 1890s.** This row of cottages at Cootham was at the end of the lane beside Cootham Hall and s very sub-standard housing. Father Basil Jellicoe, who spent his latter years in Sullington and founded the St. Richard using Society, died while the subject of their demolition was being considered.

140. **St. Richard's, Cootham, 1977.** After the death of Father Jellicoe, his cherished scheme of re-housing these people went ahead. The Long Row was demolished and these new cottages had their first tenants in 1937.

141. **Cootham Hall and Pond, 1890s.** This photograph was taken from the (now) Pulborough Road. The cottage jus[t] beyond the hall is Flansham Cottage, and the Long Row can be seen looking very dilapidated.

142. **Cootham Hall and Pond, 1977.**

The Water-Corn Mill

43. The Bine-Mill and Pond. This is the corn-mill and pond behind the village. The hill behind was called Spion Kop fter the Boer War.

144. Car Park, Pond and Mill Field Development, 1977. An incredible transformation. The car park is beside the new Public Library in North Street, and the re-constructed ornamental pond can be seen to the right. Spion Kop and the fields are completely built over. In the 1970s efforts were made to preserve the old mill, but quite suddenly it was demolished. The flats on the opposite side of the pond (with the white strip) occupy the mill site.

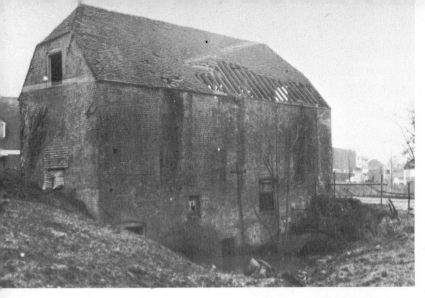

Last Days of the Bine-Mill

145. In the early 1970s. The old mill is in a sadly derelict state. Behind it is the new shopping precinct and the Book Sho on the extreme right on the other side of the High Street (the white shop). Staring into its empty windows on the left are the new houses of the Mill Field development.

146. A good view of the water wheel and conduits, in the last stages of its life. It was an overshot wheel, driven by water pouring on to it from the pond and emptying into a small mill stream which went back into the Stor further down.

147. Old Mill, New Pond and Houses. These new flats seem to be elbowing the old mill out of the way, and the smart ne pond now serves only ornamental purpos The other end of the conduit that took water from the pond to the wheel can sti be seen under the wall where the lady is standing, but the water no longer rises that high.

. **Path to the Mill.** The path went through the field and over a footbridge. This picture is a continuation of the left side
he previous one (see plate 143) as can be seen by the pollarded willow between the path and the pond.

149. **Car Park and Footbridge to Stor Meadow, 1977.** The North Street car park
and bridge. This crosses a weir between the pond on the right, and the river Stor
which winds its way out to Hurston on the left.

150. **View Across Storrington.** In the foreground is the Bine-Mill and pond. The tower of the Parish Church is seen on the extreme left, and the Monastery between the trees on the right. Above the Monastery on the skyline of the downs is Rackham Clump. The picture was taken from Spion Kop.

151. **View Across Storrington, 1977.** This valley has been intensively developed in the last seven years. The church is immediately to the left of the tall aerial, but the Monastery is screened by trees. Rackham Clump on the skyline gives some clue to its location, but even the skyline has changed, marked now by many small trees and bushes.

Events in Storrington

152. **The Flower Show, 1906.** Prize-giving. The Hon. Miss Curzon of Parham is sitting at the table distributing prizes and the Rector's little daughter sits with Mr. and Mrs. Erskine of Greyfriars House. The Flower Show was first tried in Storrington in 1850 and continued until 1875, when it lapsed. It was re-started in 1905, and this picture shows that it was a very popular event.

153. The Flower Show, 1957. General View. This is the view of the recreation ground that met the eye coming through the entrance on Show Day. There are people everywhere, the large marquee, smaller tents for teas, sideshows etc., and the roped-off enclosure for various outdoor events such as baby shows, dog shows and sports. There was also a fair with swings, roundabouts, and all the usual attractions over towards what is now the Hurston housing estate.

154. The Flower Show, 1967. This is the scene inside the big marquee when the exhibitors have finished arranging their entries and all is awaiting the arrival of the judges. The show continued annually (except in wartime) and as this picture shows, it drew nearly 1,000 individual entries in two sections, horticultural and handicraft. This is the horticultural end of the show tent.

155. The Flower Show, 1972. Just one of the handicraft tables with part of the massive art entry in the background. To the left of this table there was another run, taken up with cookery, preserves and wine. On the other side of the art stands were flower arrangements, children's entries and photography. The prize-winning model of Henry VIII was made in all its details from a copy of a Holbein portrait which hangs in Parham House, and was made by the author.

156. Children's Tea-Party, 1906. Hayfield teas were a very popular event in the children's summers. In this one, the little girl who wrote this card asks her auntie if she can find her in the picture. She gives the clue that she is wearing a hat with 'rooshing' on it. The field where these children are enjoying their tea is now a part of the Spierbridge housing estate.

157. (*below*) **Haymaking in the Church Meadow, 1908.** This is in the church meadow with the rectory in the background. The little girl fifth from the right in the front sitting cross-legged is the rector's daughter, and the next but one to her in the dark beret is another well-known Storringtonian — Miss Florrie Greenfield.

Brownies, Scouts and Guides

8. 8th April 1931. The First Storrington Brownie Pack attend the wedding of Miss Helen Fuller, who was the second Brown Owl of the pack.

159 & 160. **lst Storrington Brownies, 1961.** Here the Brownies enjoy outdoor activities in the field behind the Guide H
This field is now just another part of the housing estate, and has had intensive building on it.

61. 1st Storrington Scout Troop, 1907-8. The new troop boasts many familiar village names. *Back Row*, left to right: Harry Cole, Norman Towse, Frank Becksfield, Henry Elms, ? , Henry Zwallen. *Middle Row*: Harry Moon (the boy with the bike outside the bakery in plate 74), Hugo Zwallen, Ray Moon, Jack Linfield. *Front Row*: ? Compton, Redvers Stringer, Walter Atfield, Reg Roy, ? , Charles Stringer.

162. 23 October 1942. The Chief Guide, Lady Baden-Powell, shakes hands with leader Lois Pitts as she greets the guard-of-honour. Behind her are Divisional Commissioners Mrs. Ravenscroft and Miss A. MacDonald. The Chief Guide was attending a conference of Guiders and Commissioners, and told the 300-strong guard-of-honour that she was 'glad to see you are carrying on your work so keenly in my old Sussex'. Lady Baden-Powell had made a 6,000-mile journey and said that it was good to come back to this country and see the flag still flying. 'I expected to see the people half-starved', she went on, 'but I find you still keeping your peckers up in spite of this war'.

Activities in the High Street

163.   The Duke of Norfolk leads the Sussex Territorials through Storrington about 1905. The carrier's cart in the Square provides a group of children with a grandstand view, and flags hang from windows.

Life in 1906. The bakers outside Moon's stop their work for a moment to pose for the camera, and Mr. Rapley also ses on the ladder, where he is engaged in painting the *Half Moon*. Between The Elders and the Capital and Counties k is the entrance to a small paddock where Abner Soffe built The Homestead two years later.

5. **The Anchor Corner, 1909.** The Duke of Norfolk and the Territorials visited Storrington en route to the camp at lington. There was an outdoor concert in the evening, and these folk wait in anticipation of the entertainment. The age is decked with flags. There are some interesting old buildings in this picture which have not survived. The old tage next to the *Anchor*, the blacksmith's next door, the cartshed just beyond the stream, the stables for Flatt's ind Moon's bakery in the Co-op yard. Next to the tallest shop on the left with its three huge windows upstairs (the tre one is no longer there) is a space where a half-timbered house was built — it is now Tucker, the Estate Agent, was not built until the year after this picture was taken. The meadow beside the stream on the right was full of d flowers, according to older people who remember.

Entertainment in the Square

166. (*above*) **The Storrington Military Band, 1909.** The b.
give one of their popular concerts in the Square, with Mulb
House behind them. This was a period of great success and
enthusiasm from the time that Mr. Trotter, who lived at T
Abbey, bought them instruments and uniforms in 1904, ar
maintained his great interest until the outbreak of World W

167. **Morris Dancers, 1 May 1955.** These are the West
Chiltington Morris Dancers, who kept up this old custom
many years.

On 2 Wheels

Start of Motor Cycle Race, 1907-8. Mr. H. W. Slaughter and Mr. A. Crowhurst (the blacksmith) line up their machines at the bottom of the hill, West Street. The building behind them now sells furnishing fabrics, but at this time was a cycle shop. Norman Towse jokingly lines up his second-hand cycle (for which he paid 9d!) with the racers. bike, incidentally, had solid tyres. The other cyclist is Dr. Lee's chauffeur.

Treasure Hunt, 1925. Cyclists line up at the west end of The Square for the start of a treasure hunt.

Building

170.   The Building of Eastbrook, 1906.

171.   **Hammering in the First Peg, 1934.** This is the site of the new rectory, the third, on the Glebe field. It was built after the sale of the Church Street rectory to the Chanctonbury R.D.C. in 1933. Mrs. Faithfull performs the ceremony, watched by the Rector, Rev. Richard Faithfull (her son), Miss Elizabeth Faithfull, her daughter and their friends.

The Great War

March to the Peace Thanksgiving, July 1919. This was a spontaneous event in which the people of Storrington all ~~red~~ at the Parish Church, regardless of their own religious beliefs. They are seen here, led by the band, marching ~~wards~~ along West Street past the wall of the Glebe field, where the child in the white dress is standing. The building ~~nd~~ the band is a blacksmith's.

Muster of Red Cross Nurses and Troops, 1919. The Red Cross nurses and troops gather before the grand muster. ~~commandant~~ in the dark uniform is Mrs. Henderson, and beside her is Miss Bartelott. In the background is the ~~lic~~ Church. This impressive group of ladies was recruited from Storrington and West Chiltington.

174. The Schoolchildren, 1919. The children of the village have their own welcome for their fathers, brothers, uncles and cousins. 'The children welcome home their heroes who bring them victory and peace', says their garlanded banner. The poles are held by Boy Scouts, and the dark-suited gentleman is their schoolmaster, Mr. Rhoden.

175. (*below*) **The Muster in the Square, 1919.** The village people watch as the various groups muster for the celebratio the troops, the Red Cross nurses, the band gathered by the l post. Many local men joined the Sussex Yeomanry. There ar flags everywhere now that the war is over. Norman Towse, n in uniform, drives a trap to bring the less agile Storringtonia to see the celebrations.

War Veterans and Roll of Honour. Many village families are represented in this group of servicemen, posing by the of Honour. Gilbert, Stocker, Stringer, Edwards. It had been hoped that one board would have been enough to accom- ate the names of the fallen, but sadly, it was soon realised that two more would be needed. And for those Storrington- who are still with us, or who remember the village's contribution to the war effort, standing at the back left to right are, bby' Stringer, ? , Martin Stringer, Bert Peto, George Rice of the *Half Moon*, George Stocker, Mark Gilbert from Stubbs' shop, and 'Bunny' Edwards. Seated in the middle are Reg Roy (last seen in Scout uniform), Arthur Elms, Alf Atfield, Ellis, one of the Storrington Bus drivers, and Harry Gilbert. The front row are Jimmy Horton, ? , ? , Norman Towse ? Newman.

Dedication of the War Memorial, 1921. Another inter-denominational event that brought the village together. This he dedication of their war memorial. The Rev. A. Faithfull on the right, the two churchwardens Jesse Johnson and Allen on the far left, Mrs. King of Fryern and in front of her, Miss Petre who is reading. Mr. Adsett of the *Worthing tte* is making notes beside the memorial.

178. (*overleaf*) **Unveiling the Roll of Honour, 1921.** Not all of the men came home. Here the villagers watch as the notice board framing the Roll of Honour is unveiled. Boy Scouts line the route and bus and coach passengers have a grand-stand view. The specially-designed board hung on the wall of the Market Room next to *The White Horse* Hotel. Unfortunately, it seems to have been lost or mislaid when the wall was painted and it was taken down.

Fire!

179. Fire at Abingworth House, 18 January 1910. This was the residence of Mr. Stanley Peach, a London architect. Abingworth House dated back to Henry VII although most of it was of the Queen Anne period. Successive owners had extensively altered and added to it, and Mr. Peach had added a one-storey wing containing a dining-room and library whe₁ he took the house in 1904. The fire broke out in the early hours and was discovered by a maid going downstairs to light ₁ kitchen fire. Mrs. Peach and her son (Mr. Peach was in London), their guests and servants escaped in their nightclothes, a₁ the flames were soon visible for miles around. Farm workers fought with buckets of water, whilst Abel Towse covered th distance to Steyning to fetch the brigade in twenty minutes. They turned out with their manual engine in three-quarters an hour. The roof collapsed before their arrival. Later, the Horsham Brigade brought their steam engine, but by noon onl the bare walls and the new wing remained.

180. Chanctonbury House, 1977. Wednesda 4 May. A strange sequel to the story of Chanctonbury House, which occurred whilst this b₁ was in preparation. The caretaker, Mr. Farha₁ going to work on the morning of the 4th, fou the reception hall full of smoke. He called th₁ Storrington Fire Brigade, who were on the sc₁ in two-and-a-half minutes — a far cry from th₁ headlong gallop from Steyning which used to bring the brigade! Even so, the brigades from Billingshurst, Steyning and Findon were also needed. The fire began in the records' store a₁ burned for some time before discovery. Irrep₁ able records and papers were lost, going back time to before the 1930s, when the Chancto₁ bury Council bought the old Rectory. A poig₁ moment came during the morning, when fire₁ from the Storrington Brigade stood at attenti in Church Street as the funeral cortege of Mr. Rolie Greenfield, their former fire chief, pass on its way to the Parish Church. The firemen planned to form a guard of honour at the fu₁ but their duties prevented them. In the pictu₁ Storrington firemen take a welcome tea-break the fire is safely under control. Seated on the parapet, right, is Storrington Station-officer

John Linfield. The steps and the front door of the offices are behind them, the wall of the old rectory building to the ri₁ and the offices to the left, the new part affected by the fire.

181, 182 & 183. This shop, as pictures throughout the book show, underwent many changes in its appearance. At the time of the fire, it was serving a double purpose as R. Vine's Radio and Electrical shop and F. G. Bryant's Coal Office. The fire is thought to have started in the shop window and then swept up the front of the building. This happened between 8.30 and 9.00 a.m. on a Sunday morning. The main fire-fighters at this time were soldiers stationed in the area and, in the dark uniforms, men of the Auxiliary Fire Service. During the War, Storrington's A.R.P. headquarters were situated in the old cottage at the back of this shop. The only access (other than through the shop!) was along the side passage between the dairy and this shop, round the back of the building and thus into 'H.Q.'.

Dramatic Society

184. **The 100th Production, 1967.** A scene from 'Berkeley Square'. The Dramatic Society was started in 1907 but its real history seems to date back to just after World War I, about 1922. After another short break it got going in 1929 with plays, gradually building up a reputation which consistently achieved good Press reports. Their 100th production was a play which spanned 100 years. Members of the cast in this photograph are, back row from the left: Tessa Wigg, Rod Bowley, P. MacAnally, Rosemary Blackman, Frances Milner. In front are Lena Tyson and Pat Leonard.

185. **Ghost Scene From 'A Murder Has Been Arranged', 1970.** This production also gave the cast an opportunity to come to grips with costume parts. These Tudor characters are, left to right: Rita Belsey, Frances Milner, Diana Waring, Dot Reid, Rod Bowley. Bernard Crabbe was to have taken part in the production, but sadly, he died during rehearsals.

Carnival

Storrington Carnival 1976. This fund-raising event is held annually, organised by the Chanctonbury Lions, and ...lving as many local organisations as can take part. This is the parade through the High Street, with the Air Training ...os' float. They have put the chequered signals of an airfield landing system on the sides, and a large 'radio' and aerial on ...of their minibus. The 2464 Squadron is a highly technological unit, and radio is one of their main activities. The cadet ...ing pace with the minibus is Lynton Bell.

Parham Point-to-Point, 9 April 1960. The Horsham and Crawley hounds put on a fine display at this meeting. This ...t-to-point was started about 25 years ago and continues to draw the crowds.

188. **Rogation Procession, 1946.** The Bishop of Chichester, The Rt. Rev. G. K. A. Bell, the rector of Storrington, Rev. W. G. Frostick and his curate, Rev. G. F. Farnsworth lead this annual Procession. It includes the choir, Girl Guides, Brownies, and members of the public with their dogs and prams. The procession walked to the school for the reading of a lesson, and then on through the village, stopping at various points to sing hymns and offer prayers.

189.   The rogation procession starts off from the parish church, led by the choir. At the top of the steps is Bishop Bell.

191.   After turning right into West Street, top of the hill, led by Mr. E. Davis carrying

190. The procession reaches the north end of Church Street, its tail stretching back to the Council Offices.

has now reached the
...al cross.

192. They are now passing the north end of the Glebe field beside Rectory Road.

193. (*above*) **20 June 1959.** A long impressive procession winds its way through the main High Street, led by the processional cross. Here, children of the Convent Schools walk in tableaux groups.

194. (*left*) **Statue of our Lady of England.** The heart of the procession, the statue, is driven in a flower-decked car; followed by the Bishop. Keeping a friendly eye on the proceedings is the unmistakable figure of the village policeman, Constable Tom Wright.

195. (*above*) **Solemn Crowning.** The Rt. Rev. Cyril Cowderoy, Bishop of Southwark, places the crown on the head of the statue.

196. (*left below*) **Te Deum Laudamus.** The close of the service.

197. Funeral of Col. Ravenscroft, 1952. The colonel leaves The Abbey, his home for nearly 30 years, for the last time. His coffin, draped with a Union Jack, is pulled on a farm cart to the Parish Church opposite his gates. Col. Ravenscroft was spoken of as the 'fairy god-father of the village', and his generosity and active interest can be traced in many amenities and in the church. His name is perpetuated in the southernmost Council estate of the village, on land to the west of The Abbey.

Produce Market

198. Storrington Produce Market in the 1950s. This picture was taken when the regular Friday market was held in the forecourt of Mulberry House near the (then) Bus Station.

199. Storrington Produce Market in 1961. The market moved to this new position in 1960, where it remained for 10 years. When the Bus Station area was developed, the market made its third move and is now held in the Village Hall.

200. (*above*) **W.I. Bulb Show, 2 March 1957.** The judges cast critical eyes on the Flower Arranging section of the show.

201. (*right*) Cup Winner Miss P. Penn with runners-up Mrs. Martin and Mrs. May.

202. (*left*) **Christmas Party, 1958.** Miss A. E. Protheroe cuts the cake sent to them all the way from Mirani in Queensland, Australia. The W. I. has world-wide links, and they keep in regular contact.

No.1 Bus Service

203, 204 & 205. The No.1 Bus Service. Until the last few years, buses running between Worthing—Storrington—Pulborough carried the distinctive number 1 on their destination boards. There is an interesting story attached to this, because Storrington did have the first bus service. In 1904, the *Sussex Motor Road Car Company* came into being, with the object of covering some cross-country routes not served by the railway. An entry in Mrs. Faithfull's diary for the time records that on Tuesday, 8 November 1904, the service was inaugurated with a trial run to *Warnes Hotel* in Worthing. The passengers, including the Rector and Mrs. Faithfull, were given lunch at *Warnes* by Mr. Erskine of Greyfriars, one of the new company's directors.

The first two steam buses charged fares from Pulborough as follows: Mare Hill, 2d., Wiggonholt Common, 3d., Coot 6d., Storrington, 9d., Washington, 1s. 0d., Findon, 1s. 6d., Worthing, 1s. 9d. By 1910, the *Worthing Motor Services* had succeeded the *Sussex Motor Road Car Company*, and this amalgamated with the *Brighton, Hove and Preston United Omnibus Co.* and the *London and South Coast Haulage Co.* to form the *Southdown* on 1 April 1915.

In the first picture (*above*) dated 1905, 'One of the new motor cars' attracts admiring attention outside the *Half Moon*.

In the second picture (*opposite page above*) the new motor buses again draw admiring onlookers outside *The White Horse Hotel* in 1905.

The last picture is of great interest. The best date that can be given is pre-1918. The bus itself is one of the original ones in the *Southdown* fleet, taken over when they were formed in 1915. It is certainly the oldest vehicle in the fleet that they know, and has a 1904 Milnes-Daimler body. The driver in conversation in the Square is Mr. Pearson. At this time and for many years afterwards, the bus terminus was in The Square.

A new bus station was built behind the Colonnade in 1953, and this was demolished to make way for a large new terminus in its present site on the Mill Field development in 1970.

THE NEW T.
MOTOR BUSES
AT
STOULTO.

206. **The 'Milk' Bus, 1913.** Driven by Mr. Pearson, the bus makes a stop at Sullington cross-roads. The milk churn can be seen beside him. The bus is a 1912 Straker Squire, part of the original *Southdown* fleet with the fleet number 29. It was aquired from *Worthing Motor Services*. In its *Southdown* career, it had a Dodson body and was a 36-seat double decker.

207. **Storrington Bus Garage, 1975.** This picture brings the bus story up-to-date, and the picture is of historical interest. Three of the fleet are parked — 133 (BUF/133/C), 204 (KUF/204/F) and 208 (KUF/208/F). This garage is believed to b the oldest *Southdown* garage still in use. When taller buses came into service, the building was not altered. Instead, the n buses were accommodated by lowering the floor-level. As the destination boards show, we have lost our proud no.1 servi and are now 201. BUF/133/C, as its number shows, is now a veteran of the fleet and due for retirement.

Outings

8. The First Charabanc, 1910. This is the regular outing to Worthing, a pleasure trip which ran weekly. The charabanc, ...istered in the Isle of Wight, belongs to the *Worthing Motor Services* and had replaced a four-in-hand which used to make ... trip. The gentleman with the horse and cart was making his regular delivery of drinks from Fryco.

209. **Cootham Sunday School Outing, 1920.** The attractions of a charabanc outing have grown, and it needs three vehic
to take the party to their destination. The left-hand one is a 1919 Tillings Steven TS3, with a Harrington 32-seat body. T
right-hand one is a Leyland.

210. **Choir Outing, 1930.** The members of Storrington Church Choir fill this charabanc for their annual outing.

211 & 212.   The date of these pictures is August 1975, but the bus and the costumes reflect life nearly half a century before. The occasion was the 900th Anniversary of Chichester Cathedral, an event celebrated by a pageant of Sussex villages. Miss E. Gray, the chairman of the Parish Council, formed a committee of local organisations in Sullington and Storrington. Their plan was formulated to commemorate Storrington's historic no.1 bus route. This grand old 1929 Leyland Titan TD1, 51-seater was supplied by the *Southdown,* and villagers whose ages ranged from three to 75 years turned up in Edwardian costumes to ride in the bus to Chichester. Two well-known ladies in the first picture, Mrs. Eddie Greenfield and Miss Florence Greenfield leave Jasmine Cottage at the eastern end of the village, dressed in impressive 'widow's weeds' to join the bus in the Square. In the second picture, the bus and its passengers wave Union Jacks from the open top of the bus.

The White Mill

CABINET PORTRAIT

213. (*left*) **1880.** This lovely post-mill stands on a hilltop on Sullington Warren. The miller, John Quait, stands at the door. He is related by marriage to the family who own the Bakery a shop in the High Street — Moons. (See plate 74). The Quaits a run the water-mill in Chantry Lane.

214. (*below*) **1890.** This watercolour of the mill on its hillto was commissioned by John Quait. The road goes to Steyning Brewery, customers of the miller, and the old wall seen in the picture is still to be seen there. The picture is now owned by N E. Moon, grand-daughter of John Quait.

215. The mill stands like a sentinel as sheep graze on adjoining land which is now covered with houses. It stretched from Heather Way to Three Gates and back to the Warren.

The old mill is beginning to show signs of deterioration
t stands among the heather, with Chanctonbury Ring in the
:ance.

217.   The Last Stand of the Old Mill, 1911. By this
time the mill was rented by Mrs. H. Crowhurst from
Lord Leconfield. It had not worked since 1903. The
summer of 1911 was hot and dry. The gorse and
bracken on the Warren caught fire and spread rapidly
despite the efforts of many beaters. The horse-drawn
fire engine, summoned by telegram from Steyning,
galloped over at top speed, but it was too late to
save the mill. It is sad to realise that although the
disused mill was deteriorating, an appeal was already
in force in 1911 to make it safe and preserve it.

.   **The Smouldering Wreckage, 1911.** The sad remains after
fire. The gorse and peat was hot for many days and the fire
ger remained acute.

219.   The Axle of the Windmill, 1977. This is still on
the hilltop, and its size can be gauged by comparison
with Sheena Buss, who accompanied me on many of the
photographic forays for this book. This cast-iron shaft
has lain here for 66 years. It would have been installed
originally, horizontally across the upper part of the mill
and the sail bars fitted into the square slots indicated by
Sheena's hand.

Cricket

220 & 221. Storrington has a history of being a cricket-loving village, from the foundation of the cricket club in 1793.
we see a proud moment for them in 1908. The event was celebrated with a dinner, when A. E. R. Gilligan was present. T
Hammonds, a famous cricketing family, were also residents of Storrington.

222. **Comic Cricket, 1910.** Th
game has not always been a sole
event. Here, the band on its rais
platform is about to play for da
cing. This picture is taken on th
recreation ground looking N.E.,
towards where the Spierbridge
Estate now stands.

223. **Comic Cricket, 1919.** Any
excuse is siezed upon for a comic
match. This one is part of the
peace celebrations after the Great
War. It was played between teams
of ladies and gentlemen — the
ladies using bats and the men
sticks! They pose outside The
Elms.

Hounds and Meets

At the Rectory, 1905. The Rev. A. F. Faithfull was a lover of hunting. Here the hounds call at the Rectory during
⸱rcise. The Rector's daughter in her white dress and shady hat watches them. Behind the hounds on the left is her father,
⸱ Arthur F. Faithfull.

225. *(overleaf)* **At the Abbey.** The Crawley and Horsham Foxhounds meet at the Abbey for Col. Ravenscroft's hospitalit

226. **Sullington Manor Farm, 1909.** These are the Wooddale Foot Beagles, later to become the Storrington Foot Beagles. The M.F.H. is Mr. Goff.

227. **The Craigweil Bloodhounds, 1905-6.** The Craigweil estate was at Bognor Regis, where George V spent 15 weeks convalescing from septicaemia. The hounds are pictured here by the Bine mill and pond. Mr. Stocker, who had a pack of bloodhounds, lived for a time in Mulberry House before moving to Bognor Regis.

Royal Celebrations

8. **Jubilee Tea Party for the Old Folk, 1935.** Col. Ravenscroft is in the centre of the front row. These Storringtonians gathered outside the Comrades' Hut, with the Nurses' cottages behind them.

229. **Coronation, 1953.** This was the Saturday afterwards. The children watch Punch and Judy on the green of Warren Hamlet. 'The Queen' is now Mrs. Barbara Burch, grand-daughter of Abner Soffe. The view is towards Water Lane where the Industrial Estate has mushroomed in these past 25 years.

The Silver Jubilee 1977

230. The Public Library staged an exhibition for the week. This was the display board in the entrance vestibule where major attractions were advertised.

231. The flags go up. Church Street 'dressed overall' for Jubilee week. Many of the traders wore red-white-and-blue dress in keeping with the spirit of the week.

232. (*right*) The parish church contributed by staging a 'Village Heritage' exhibition and by making a floral picture which was displayed outside the north door. The Rector, Rev. John Norman, seen here with his wife working on the picture, was previously parish priest of Ashford-in-the-Water in the Peak District, and brought the well-dressing technique with him to create this beautiful tribute, which was much admired. The picture was built up with flower petals pressed on wet clay, and the richly coloured panels of scarlet (geranium), purple (periwinkle) and cream (syringia) were framed with green parsley. The gold orbs and sceptres at the sides and the crown at the top were filled with glittering buttercup petals from the glebe field, collected by Brownies, and the two bells were silver cineraria leaves.

233. Inside the church, visitors study the 'Village Heritage' exhibition of old paintings, postcards, church registers and a facsimile Domesday Book open at the page where the two manors of 'Storchestone' and 'Estorchetone' are listed, together with the church. The figures at the altar display church vestments, and the flower arrangements were designed to match the colours of the vestments.

234.   Monday 6 June. The Southdown Gliding Club held an open day at their Parham Landing Ground, with a fête and exhibitions. Here, a glider can be seen coming in for a landing, with others parked. The trailers to the right house gliders in transit.

235.   Monday 6 June ended with a bonfire on Chantry, together with a barbecue and hot dog stand. The evening was bitterly cold, and the moment when Storrington's bonfire joined the chain of fires along the downs was greatly appreciated by the large crowd.

6. Tuesday, 7 June. Storrington Horticultural & Handicrafts Society held a special Jubilee Mini-Show in the Village Hall.
Smith, the secretary, is seen in conversation with Mr. E. Dougal in this view down the main hall.

237. Storrington could not let such a special occasion go by without celebrating in cricket. On Wednesday evening,
June (the one glorious sunny evening in a cold and dull week) Storrington Cricket Club staged a match with
Storrington Football Club. The batsman at the main road end is just being dismissed by the bowler.

238. On Friday, 10 June, it was the turn of the Trinity Methodist Church, who decorated their church with flower arrangements and held a coffee morning in the rooms behind the church.

239. The week ended with a light-hearted Dog Gymkhana on the Recreation Ground. The judge has just presented the overall winners with their trophies.